BUCKS COUNTY

BUCKS COUNTY

PHOTOGRAPHS OF EARLY ARCHITECTURE

BY AARON SISKIND

TEXT BY WILLIAM MORGAN

Published for THE BUCKS COUNTY HISTORICAL SOCIETY *by* HORIZON PRESS

Library of Congress Catalog Card Number 74-19773
ISBN 0-8180-1416-4
Printed in the United States of America

CONTENTS

THE EARLY ARCHITECTURE OF BUCKS COUNTY

THIS book of photographs by Aaron Siskind is about the early architecture of Bucks County, Pennsylvania. Bucks County's historical and cultural legacy is greater than its 600 square-mile size would suggest, and these buildings constitute a major contribution to the area's unique heritage. After all a county is a geo-political unit, but Bucks is one of a handful of the more than 3,000 counties in the United States that commands recognition beyond state borders. The name evokes images of William Penn, the American Revolution, summer theater, landscape painters, pastoral countryside, and, not least of all, the fieldstone houses and barns that are the main protagonists in Siskind's essay.

From the beginning, Bucks County's important future role was assured by geography. The Falls of the Delaware, just below Trenton, marks the boundary between piedmont and tidewater, as well as the end of hopes for the European explorers who ventured up the Delaware in search of a Northwest Passage. Since it straddled coast and plain, the county could not help but grow; the pre-settlement Indian trails, the later coach routes running between New York and Philadelphia, and its present central location in the Boston-to-Washington Megalopolis, define the crossroads nature of Bucks County.

Its situation as a crossroads was to make Bucks County strategically important during the Revolutionary War, especially after Washington's retreat following the disastrous Long Island campaign in August of 1776. The Delaware provided Washington and his beleaguered army with a momentary barricade behind which he was able to plan the successful attack on the Hessian garrison at Trenton—a turning point in the War for Independence. The dangerous Christmas Night river crossing was later immortalized in the well-known painting by Emanuel Leutze. The event was further commemorated by the establishment of Washington Crossing State Park, in which is preserved the Thompson-Neely House, sometimes claimed as the place where Washington planned his attack and where Thomas Paine wrote "Common Sense."

Another key reason for Bucks County's strategic importance was its agricultural bounty. One of the three original counties in William Penn's Quaker Commonwealth, Bucks attracted Germans, Scotch-Irish and other settlers, including Quakers, and by the Revolution it could claim some of the richest farmland in the Colonies, with wheat its principal cash crop. The wheat, oats, corn and potatoes of its fields made it a potential commissary for both the British and American armies. It was this rich agricultural yield that raised Bucks to a level of prosperity that allowed for the replacing of the earlier log cabins with the stone houses that were to become the County's signature.

As 20th-century Bucks County developed beyond the farming economy, the lawyer, archaeologist, anthropologist, and Doylestown native, Henry Chapman Mercer (1856-1930), became concerned about the preservation of the stone houses, the log cabins, and all the other physical evidence of our pre-industrial society. After years of wide-ranging archaeological and natural history exploration, Dr. Mercer began directing his scholarly research to the area around his Doylestown home. Wisely believing that the utensils and implements of everyday use and labor give as much insight into the nature of a people as do more conventional historical documents, Mercer began amassing many of the tools developed in rural America. This gentleman-scholar also recognized the intrinsic importance of the objects themselves as the artistic expression of their makers; and this in turn led to pioneering publications such as *The Bible in Iron* (1914), a monograph on Pennsylvania

German stoveplates and firebacks. This study of the Pennsylvania-German contribution (making Mercer one of the earliest champions and collectors of American Folk Art) included pottery manufacture and decoration, a craft whose preservation necessitated his reviving it.

Mercer's Moravian Pottery and Tile Works, using local clay and a unique glaze made from a recipe of William de Morgan (potter and novelist of the William Morris circle of English handicraft revivalists), produced tiles that received international acclaim, as well as the grand prize at the Louisiana Purchase Exposition in St. Louis in 1904 and a gold medal from the American Institute of Architects.

In 1897 Mercer first showed some of the many tools and utensils he had collected. In order to house this extensive and ever-expanding collection, which he called "Tools of the Nation Maker," Mercer designed, built, and donated to The Bucks County Historical Society, a large reinforced concrete museum. (Mercer's nearby house, "Fonthill," built in 1907-12, and the Moravian tile factory also use Mercer's advanced reinforced concrete construction.) Interesting as the 115-foot-high, seventy-room structure is architecturally, it is the collection housed in its one million cubic foot area that places this building beyond the range of almost every other "county" museum in the country. Like Bucks County itself, the museum collection is of more than local interest. In Mercer's words, the tools and objects rescued from oblivion "are larger than the history of our county and even larger than the history of the United States"; they are of "world-wide significance."

Despite his desire for a broader collection (as was illustrated by his funding of an expedition to China in 1921 for the study and documentation of old tools in that country, as well as his initiating a collection of crafts and religious objects from West Africa), the matrix of the Historical Society collection was to be composed of local artifacts. And so Mercer spent the last three decades of his life personally collecting and documenting the physical reminders of Bucks County's history.

Years before the formation of an Historic American Buildings Survey to make measured drawings and do historical studies of old houses and public structures, Henry Mercer filled several notebooks with invaluable information concerning Bucks County architecture. These notes have become a chief source on the subject. Much of the data he gathered went into two publications, *The Dating of Old Houses* (1923) and *Ancient Carpenters' Tools* (1929), both of which remain classics in the field of architectural restoration. Mercer did not, however, write an architectural history of Bucks County.

And while certain houses, such as Pennsbury Manor and Andalusia, have appeared in general books on American buildings, a definitive history of Bucks County's architecture remains to be written.

Perhaps the closest work approaching this goal was Charlotte Stryker's "Colonial Architecture of Bucks County." This manuscript developed from her study of architectural history with Talbot Hamlin at Columbia University and was intended for publication. Sharing Mercer's broader outlook, Mrs. Stryker wished to present "these survivals of the past age not only as sticks and stones but in terms of the way of life which built and used them." In so presenting the buildings she tells of the region, its agricultural prosperity as the bread-basket of Philadelphia, and of the Quaker settlement, along with the predominance of Friends' ideas and influences long after the Quakers themselves were out-numbered by Germans, Scotch-Irish, and other land hungry settlers.

Aaron Siskind and Charlotte Stryker met through a mutual friend in New York, and as he had been photographing Bucks County buildings on his own, they informally agreed to join forces, using certain of his pictures to illustrate her text.

In choosing the title "Colonial Architecture of Bucks County," Charlotte Stryker did not fall into the trap of using "colonial" to refer to what we know of more properly as Georgian. She felt that the term was appropriate to Bucks County (and to the buildings of the whole Delaware Valley region), for the religious and agricultural determinants produced something that might be better called "a country style of building rather than architecture," a vernacular style similar to that of colonial Pennsylvania as a whole. It is generally a conservative as well as an additive building style. There is very little stylistic evolution; houses tended to grow larger when the standard of living permitted, rather than be replaced or remodeled according to more up-to-date fashions.

The sources for Bucks County architecture are undoubtedly English. While German settlers did contribute the two-story barn, for their dwellings they adopted the local vernacular. While owing something to the influence of Philadelphia, the colonies' political and cultural capital, the relationship between country and city styles was not dissimilar to that which prevailed in England at the time. Just as the buildings of London's aristocracy followed the Renaissance fashion as introduced into England by Inigo Jones and later formalized by Sir Christopher Wren, Philadelphia erected such Georgian monuments as the State House (Independence Hall) and Christ Church. Be-

frontal, straightforward way of handling them, demonstrates his respect for the "reality" of the picture plane—an understanding that the print, as surely as the painter's canvas, is what it is: a flat, two-dimensional surface. Siskind, like Claude Monet or Jackson Pollock, is not interested in presenting us with the illusion of a three-dimensional picture window, but rather the reverse; the development of his work has been toward even greater non-objectivity and flatness.

While 1943-45 is usually given as the period in which Siskind developed his individual approach to transformation of subject matter into non-perspectival picture plane, it was a development that had its genesis with the Bucks County essay. By the time of Siskind's summer sojourns on Cape Ann (1944-45), his works became so abstract that subject matter often was not recognizable and not really of importance. By the 1950's Siskind's photography found a sympathetic audience among the circle of abstract painters that formed the "New York School," such artists as Barnett Newman, Willem de Kooning and Franz Kline.

However, immediately following the quiet beauty of the Bucks County project, Siskind contributed to a number of documentary projects that were at once more urban and, as their titles suggest, more socially oriented: "Harlem Document," "Dead End: The Bowery," "Portrait of a Tenement," "St. Joseph's House: the Catholic Worker Movement" (all for the Photo League, 1936-39) and his own "Most Crowded Block in the World" (1939).

That Siskind's work is often cited as a major influence on photographic aesthetics since the mid-1950's is attributable both to his mastery as a photographer and his vocation as a teacher. Siskind began as an instructor of English in New York City junior high schools, but his duties have more importantly included a post (and later chairmanship of the Photography Department) at the Institute of Design of the Illinois Institute of Technology in Chicago (where he directed a photographic survey of the architecture of Louis Sullivan), and his current post at Rhode Island School of Design. In the summer of 1951 Siskind taught at Black Mountain College in North Carolina, one of the most radical and exciting educational experiments ever undertaken in America.

Of the one hundred or so photographs of Bucks County taken by Siskind, Charlotte Stryker selected seventy-eight to illustrate her planned text. These she arranged generally according to chronology and type, such as early stone and log houses, meeting houses, mills and barns, bridges and school houses, all interspersed with exterior details (mainly doorways) and some interiors. Of perhaps greater interest to us are the two score pictures that Siskind culled and arranged for exhibition at the Delaware Gallery in New Hope in February of 1945. Entitled "Old Houses of Bucks County," the show consisted of forty-six prints mounted on ten panels, each illustrating a certain house, a grouping of similar buildings or details, or a general theme. While individual photographs appeal to the contemporary viewer on artistic grounds, the panels reflect Mrs. Stryker's didactic intentions.

One whole panel is devoted to William Penn's brick manor house of 1683, Pennsbury, selected to show the early English influence. Though it does show an almost feudal manor complete with outbuildings and dependencies, the historical value is somewhat lessened by the fact that Pennsbury is a conjectural reconstruction of the late 1930's.

Of greater historical value is the panel illustrating the growth of the "typical Bucks County house." The one-part, one-story stone cabin in Riegelsville is an example of the earliest type of dwelling (later used as an outbuilding), and we see how the two-part stone house (Richborough) evolved into three parts (Thompson-Neely House, 1701-89) and eventually into the four-part house (Bye House, near Lahaska, begun 1701). To show masonry construction, two ruined houses are included; the decaying aspect of the one near Jamison must have appealed to Siskind, and he was no doubt fascinated by the planar ambiguity in the remaining portion of a shattered windowpane.

The Parry Mansion of 1784 and the Ingham House of 1747, both in New Hope, are subjects of entire panels and both are excellent examples of the fully developed Bucks County stone house. The Benjamin Parry House (erected by the owner of the "New Hope Mills" from which the town took its name, and recently restored, is serving as the headquarters of the New Hope Historical Society), with its Philadelphia style dormers, simple quoining and splayed stone lintels, and the Ingham house (built by Jonathan Ingham and home of his grandson, Samuel D. Ingham, a member of Congress and later Secretary of the Treasury in Andrew Jackson's cabinet), with its fully panelled parlor wall and external proportions, show the influence of the Georgian style. Yet a Doylestown stone dwelling of almost a hundred years later with its Philadelphia coved porch hood and town house plan shows how conservative Bucks County was architecturally.

The end result of this conservative building tradition is that the county has a large number of structures in its own specific regional style. But this was achieved at the exclusion of the more contemporary architectural fashion, namely the national styles found almost everywhere else in early nineteenth-century America. Except for an occasional picturesque gable gleaned from the very popular pattern books of Andrew Jackson Downing, the Gothic Revival has few examples in Bucks County. The only "Gothic" building photographed by Siskind was the Warwick Presbyterian Church on Neshaminy Creek, and this is basically a Quaker style meeting house actually built in 1743 and gothicized in the 1850's with pointed windows, a bracketed porch, and a Tudor arched entranceway. The retardataire nature of the county's building style is further demonstrated by the dearth of Greek Revival style structures—a style that permeated almost every hamlet in the country in the 1830's and 1840's. The exceptions are to be found in Bristol—which was the county's only port, the terminus of the Delaware Canal which ran from Easton, and the county's largest town—and included one of the most magnificent Greek Revival houses in America, Andalusia.

Although it was an earlier house, Andalusia (so named because of a previous owner's trade business with the Spanish colonies in South America), was remodeled about 1833 by Thomas U. Walter, architect of Girard College in Philadelphia and later of the United States Capitol, for Nicholas Biddle, the President of the Bank of the United States and fiscal antagonist of Andrew Jackson. Biddle, an early Grecophile, was one of the few western travelers to visit Turkish-controlled Greece, and the classic hexastyle Doric portico that he commissioned draws its inspiration—at Biddle's insistence—directly from the Theseum in Athens. Along with the Biddle house, Siskind depicted a much larger, early Greek house with Ionic porticos at both ends (built near Croydon in 1819 and not nearly as archaeological as Andalusia). Built the same year as Andalusia, the Croydon house served briefly as Bristol College, a venture of the Episcopal Education Society of Pennsylvania. When photographed, the house was deteriorating and is now a virtual ruin.

Far more typical of the local style is the group comprised of the Friends Meeting House in Byberry (now in Philadelphia) and the 1709 Friends Meeting House in Bristol. Also included in this group are the Moravian schoolhouse of 1746 in Bethlehem (at that time in Bucks County) and the Mennonite Meeting House at Deep Run, exemplifying the preeminence of German settlers in the northern part of the county (German was the language of the neighboring Deep Run schoolhouse until 1850). The Deep Run house of worship, built in 1878, is not a great deal different stylistically from the Bristol example. The simplicity of these buildings is further documented by a panel devoted to the doorways of Deep Run and meeting houses and churches in Doylestown, Fallsington, New Hope and Washington Crossing.

Almost as typical of Bucks County (and perhaps more characteristic) are the barns, of which Siskind selected five. Irrespective of their erection dates, these combination wood and stone structures show their builders' overriding concern with function, their sloping hillside locations facilitating the loading and unloading of fodder. Another example of German influence, these utilitarian barns are some of Bucks County's most endearing monuments.

Characteristic of the pictures in the New Hope show is the very strong lighting, the almost crowded framing, a love of wall texture (whether wood boards in need of paint or stone walls in need of repointing), and the ability to create two dimensional abstract patterns. Nowhere is this last aspect more apparent than in the panel devoted to staircases. Even though a comparison of the multitude of balusters at Trevose and the twisting staircase with the treadles held between the stuccoed walls might be used to demonstrate stylistic differences of their respective houses, Siskind's downward looking viewpoint and the virtual non-objectivication of the stairs could almost be mistaken for Sheeler's rendition of the same subject, or perhaps even Tina Modotti's "Staircase, Mexico" of the mid 1920's.

A number of the photographs share this mixture of historical information and artistic abstraction, as well as possible references to other artists and artistic movements. The subject of "Covered Bridge over the Delaware River at Lumberville" (condemned in 1946) displaces only a small band across the horizon, assuming a secondary place to Siskind's real interest: the reflective patterns created by the Delaware Canal which stretches abruptly from the foreground. Perhaps the most revealing and arresting photograph in this respect (and one curiously not included in either the New Hope show or the Stryker manuscript) is one taken of the canal lock just below New Hope in which the precipitous vantage point—the arrangement of canal barges, lock walls, and broad areas of water—creates a near Cubist composition. Less radical, but almost as striking, is the photograph of Stover's Mill. This handsome, three-story stone example of mill architecture fills the whole frame in a manner reminiscent of Walker Evans, while the long figure standing in the doorway (the only person in the entire photographic survey) recalls the stoic, universal portraits of Paul Strand.

"Stover's Mill" was one of five pictures that formed Siskind's last panel, which was devoted to county industry—the mills that ground the grain and sawed the lumber that was sold to Philadelphia. The Maris textile mill of 1812 is another example. While the overshot wooden water wheel may seem rather quaint and old fashioned compared to the giant steel mills now on the Falls of the Delaware, the favorable conditions that invited industrial development in the eighteenth and nineteenth centuries also contributed to its further expansion in the twentieth century—eventually making the Delaware Valley one of the most highly industrialized regions in the world.

These pictures of mills are particularly poignant as well as prophetic, for the modern plants that replaced the mills in Bristol, Philadelphia and Trenton have changed Bucks County more dramatically in the last thirty years than in all the time previous (the county's population has grown from 107,700 in 1940 to 415,000 in 1970). Since Siskind's photographs were made, the population growth in the southern third of the county has all but obliterated its past; Pennsbury and Andalusia are surrounded by steel mills, railroad tracks, asphalt ribbons, neon, the world's largest car dealer, and Levittown—composed of a house type that is absolutely antithetical to all that the Bucks County vernacular tradition stands for. Siskind avoided the seamier side of man's effect on the natural environment. The photograph entitled "Neshaminy Creek" shows a pastoral scene, not unlike a Constable landscape, complete with meandering stream and cows; there is not a tract house, power line, or filling station in sight.

Siskind's photographs are valuable as an historical record, showing not only architectural and building types (such as log houses, of which there were only about twenty at the time Charlotte Stryker was writing), but countless structures that are no longer standing. The Lumberville covered bridge and many of the then ruined mills survive only through pictures, so that these photographs constitute part of our heritage.

But what has been lost in the three or more decades since these pictures were made is a Bucks County that was rural. No one would deny that there is a certain justification for growth, for change, for "progress," but the vision presented to us by Aaron Siskind through images of milk cans waiting to be picked up, a Quaker gravestone marking the resting place of a ninety-seven-year-old woman named "Charity," and barns sheltering horse-drawn wagons (who wouldn't prefer the legend "Chew Red Man Tobacco" painted on a barn to the flashing, strident neon of a hamburger stand?) has all but disappeared.

Recalling our loss through fire, time, real estate pressures, neglect and stupidity, we can be thankful for the foresight of idealists like Henry Mercer who preserved so much of our common past. And Aaron Siskind's photographs serve to remind us of the necessity and the responsibility to preserve that for which Bucks County is special and which, often by chance, remains. These pictures of the architecture of Bucks County remind us of our cultural legacy, but should not be a substitute for the physical reality of the buildings themselves.

That intelligent preservation planning is needed for Bucks County is obvious to anyone who has known the area longer than a decade, as is the case with this writer who moved across the Delaware from Mercer County, New Jersey, in 1952 to live in a stone barn that had served as a hospital for Washington's army during the Trenton campaign, and later as a studio for one of New Hope's many painters. Growing up in Bucks County gives one exposure to the artistic and literary figures that have traditionally been drawn to the area, along with a tradition of religious freedom and first-hand knowledge of a sturdy regional architecture, and therefore creates a debt not easily repaid. Let this essay be the first installment.

—William Morgan

Department of Art & Archaeology
Princeton University
June, 1974

THE PHOTOGRAPHS

27　Covered bridge, Lumberville

28   Thompson-Neely House, 1701-1789, River Road, south of New Hope (top); Barn (bottom)

29 Stream

30 Partial stone structure

31   Greek revival, 1819 (Farmers National Bank), Bristol

Canal at New Hope

35 Moravian minister's house, Bethlehem, Northampton County (facing page); Barn with hex signs (above)

Staircase, Trevose

40 Stable

41   Doorway, Newtown-Langhorne Road (left); Doorway (right)

42   Moravian Schoolhouse, 1746, Bethlehem, Northampton County

43   Covered bridge over Tohickon Creek, 1872

44   Stover Mill, Erwinna

45 Greek temple style (Bristol College), 1834, near Croydon

46 Fence

47 Stairway

Door and detail of stonework

50 Parlor fireplace, Doylestown-Philadelphia Road

51 Doorway with hex sign

52   Canal lock

53 Swartzlander House, Doylestown

54 Farmhouse

55 Neshaminy of Warwick Presbyterian Church

56   Friends Meeting House, Bristol

57   Covered bridge over Delaware at Lumberville

58   Wood barn and door

59   Row of houses, Bristol

61 Meeting House, Byberry

63 Barn door

64　Mennonite Schoolhouse, Deep Run (top); Interior of the brewhouse, Pennsbury (bottom)

65 Farmhouse

66 Stream, bridge and church

67   Kitchen fireplace, Ingham House, near New Hope

68 Barn, shed, cellar

69 Front door, Pennsbury

70   Stone barn

71   Bye House, begun in 1701, Lahaska

72   Eight-square Schoolhouse, Wrightstown Township

73   Stone building

74   Friends Meeting House, 1768, at Buckingham

75   Mill with wheel

76   Two views of the Parry House, 1784, New Hope (above and facing page)

78 Barn, Doylestown, Dublin Road

83　Spiral stair, near Carversville

89   An old house with a new roof near Washington Crossing

90   Ingham House, 1747, near New Hope

91 Two small barn doors

93 "Gargoyle," Richlandtown

94 An over-door hood, 1768, Doylestown

95   County records office before 1776 at Trevose

96 House (left); Church (right)

97   One-story log cabin, Riegelsville, Hellertown Road

98   Masonry construction, Cuttalossa Creek, River Road, north of New Hope

Mennonite Meeting House, 1878, Deep Run (top); Hip-roof house, near Richboro (bottom)

101 Wagon shed at Fallsington Friends Meeting House, Fallsington

102   Stone spring house (top); Barn at Springtown (bottom)

103 Two-story house near Newtown

105 Mill on Cuttalossa Creek, 1740

106 Interior, Pennsbury

107 Maris Mill near New Hope, 1812

108   Mennonite Schoolhouse, Deep Run (top); Parry Barn, New Hope (bottom)

109   A pent roof, Fallsington

110   Doorway, Mennonite Meeting House, Deep Run, 1878